CAPE POETRY PAPERBACKS

JEREMY REED
BY THE FISHERIES

Jeremy Reed

BY THE FISHERIES

JONATHAN CAPE
THIRTY BEDFORD SQUARE LONDON

First published 1984
Reprinted 1985
Copyright © 1984 by Jeremy Reed

Jonathan Cape Ltd
30 Bedford Square, London WC1

British Library Cataloguing in Publication Data
Reed, Jeremy
By the fisheries.
I. Title
821'.914   PR6068.E/

ISBN 0–224–02154–0

The following poems have previously appeared in other sources: 'Buoys' (*Literary Review*); 'By the Fisheries' (*Poetry Review*); 'Air' and 'Christopher Smart in Madness' (*Temenos*; 'Air' also appeared in *Waves*); 'Visiting Hours' (*Twofold*); 'Housman in Old Age', 'Rifts', 'Summer', 'New Stanzas', 'The Eel', 'To Him Away', 'An Age Bereft' and 'Greek Colony' (*Straight Lines*; 'Greek Colony' also appeared in *Aquarius*); 'Conger' (*The Glasgow Magazine*); 'A Location' (Gregory Awards anthology); 'Questionably' (Enitharmon Press); 'John Clare's Journal' (Menard Press and *Labrys*); 'Surfers' (The *New Statesman*); and 'The Person from Porlock' (*London Review of Books*). Six of these poems ('The Storm', 'To Him Away', 'Conger', 'Dogfish', 'Christopher Smart in Madness' and 'Buoys') appeared in Penguin's anthology of new writing, *Firebird 3*.

Condition of Sale

Printed in Great Britain by
Thomson Litho Ltd, East Kilbride, Scotland

Contents

Composition

His red silk necktie flares, and moodily
she's turned to watch a tufted duck's apache

black head streak rival the mallard's turban
of iridescent silks, and shelducks scan

the sky's cameo in the lake. The lime
tree smells of rain – a scent come from the shine

of an old pocket in which coins have lain.
The jasmine's musty, and azaleas stain

the water madder rose. It's sharper now
the shower's build-up, and a greylag scows

for shelter. Why it is that two conflict
upon a scale of moods he can't predict

a pattern to's the puzzle, like this lake's
alphabet of V's – web-footed duck wakes

that cut the green silk to a convict's cloth
of arrows. A swan turntables a wreath

on the darkening water, and he draws
his mind back in, edging for words to thaw

a silence, cold as a quartz vein in stone,
and then she's plunging, as her opaline

necklace splits on its string – each green bead's lit
by a raindrop scoring a perfect hit.

Buoys

Punch drunk are worked over,
beleaguered by each sea's
top-spin of swell, lathered
and pitched to queasily

restabilize, they are ochre
pumpkin-heads pocked with rust shale
in a whorl of white water,
grouting like snouts in a pail

in the momentary backwash
of Atlantic welter.
To seagulls they're atolls,
to the tern flying saucers,

and obesely unsinkable,
they are a boxer's nightmare
of a face repeatedly hit
that won't black-out, but stays there.

They are bulk opposing a sea
that never stops running, markers
of dangerous shoals, their bells
warning off intruders

gruffly as farm-dogs. Herded
out across nautical charts,
they are inshore satellites,
playing their rumbustious parts

for all sea-craft. Vigilant bulls
confined to marking time,

they too in their anchorage
tug at a nose-chain,

and snore hoarsely in storm,
the sea waterbug-green,
beneath a sky black
as a cormorant's sheen.

Two I see wintering
at grass in a shipping yard,
veterans of long wars,
their grizzled tonsures hard

with resilience, awaiting
new paint, their cyclopean
eyeballs gone rusty from staring
unlidded at the ocean.

Hail on the Rebound

A fizz, and then the rush is voluble,
hail stones the size of mistletoe berries
are sieved through crevices, clicking marbles

that split, ricochet, and made angular
take off into a frenetic orbit,
lose volume and subside as frosted stars

on asphalt and grebe-crested tufts of grass.
Their cooling meets the temperature of air
that has the surface clarity of glass,

and in the pause between volleys the calm
is urgent with the singing of a thrush
whose notes test the air with the quick alarm

that flattens a cat to liquidity
so that it seems possessed only of eyes.
A single stone falls intermittently –

its rap's the crackle of a robin's beak
tenaciously chipping at a snail-shell,
then the note's faster, and the air vibrates

as though someone was kneading sacks of grain
before they split and poured into a yard.
This time I rush outside into the lane,

my knuckles stung by the dactylic ring
of dice-sized ice-cubes bouncing back knee-high
from the crown of the road and scuttering

to icy corners. They're like mushrooms grown
up instantaneously before one's eyes.
A sudden gust and each ice-spark is blown

back in my face: I feel my clothes catch light
with the incandescent brilliance of pearls,
and then I'm running and my eyes are bright.

Christopher Smart in Madness

They spare me Bedlam for St Luke's Shoreditch,
who am appointed heir to King David,
and fester here where rabid
cries accompany Battie's enquiry
as to madness, whence comes this divine itch
to see into the limits of the sky?
I trundle God's gold ball in Satan's ditch.

They bait me like a bear. My creditors
are importuning demons who'd usurp
my episcopal claims. They hurt
my fevered head, and festinate the ague,
so that I shrink back in my noisome lair,
and crouch there, distracted, unwitting, vague.
The fire of ADORATION burns my hair.

My wife's a Moabite, a Newbery
for whom I squandered my pen in burlesque
before the angelic lyre struck
my holiness to David. Now I pray
that all hurt things are of one ministry.
Listen, the redbreast sings in February,
appointed angel to our misery.

And I am delivered from London's news,
its pettifogging brawls. Johnson alone
gives meat to a dead skeleton
of words; and came by. How his linen stank,
like mine. His strength prevents him breaking
through to the other side of reason. I drank,
before a red cloud opened in the blue,

and I prayed vociferously to God,
and bound myself to the purgative wheel
which burnt the lining of my soul.
Jubilate Agno, they'd confiscate,
except my mind's like a worm in a clod,
which cut in half can still compose, secrete,
and render consecration to David.

Cuckolded, cheated of inheritance,
I shiver here, and hear the sudden bell
of Staindrop Church. Lilac umbels
chequered the grass, the wild polyanthus,
I picked for one Anne Hope, and then in trance,
saw our heavenly marriage through stained glass.
God's voice was further then. I had distance.

And now a pauper go. My alms are words
of prophecy. God lit my candlestick's
orange and immutable wick,
but still they never see. Harping-irons
prod us to tasks, who cower here in dread,
and see rats catch the bread for which we pine,
and hungry, live upon raw gin instead.

Let Peter rejoice with the white moon fish
that's radiant in the dark, and let attend
Jesus on us, unsound of mind,
who cured Legion. My brethren here despair
of light, and must in other madhouses
repine for day; and go without repair.
I pray so loudly that the others curse.

The prison dampness comes to coat my skin
who venture in God's fire, and see the stone
on the right hand side of his throne

withheld from man. And gold within the dark,
I see the mine of Hell where the napkin
of the escaped Jesus still redly marks
the stone, and brooding on it I see Cain.

Outside it rains. I hear a horse collapse,
and men beat it ferociously with sticks.
It died. I pray God for redress
of all animal injuries. Tonight
I wept, and thought to incur a relapse,
and in his knowledge God brightened his light.
Tonight Christ's lantern swings inside this house.

By the Fisheries

The sea's translucent here, slowed to a calm
by an opposing breakwater, a form
of improvised harbour – its concrete arm

projected to oppose a running grey
current that's never still, but turns over
the way a leaf might, caught up in the spray

of a waterfall to expose markings
of jasper and lime as an underside
to galled blues, here contained as in a ring

siphoned off the channel by industry.
Here where a desalination plant churns
its outwash into a let of the sea,

and the zinc buildings of a fisheries
are cantoned above a hollow backdrop,
I stand, fishing that pooled serenity

for mullet, and watch sunlight make a star
on the shards of a broken gin bottle.
The aim's to cast wherever shadows are

composed by cloud, and not the diffusion
of one's image breaking up in water.
I watch my float's spherical orange cone

calligraphize its motion on the glare
that strikes the water like molten lead poured
into a sheet that furnaces on air,

and hangs there in a cobalt flame. A man
trundles an offal barrow to a bin,
and stands a long time with a yellow can,

staring at my immobile silhouette,
pensively tilted back into shadow,
my features guarded by a wide-brimmed hat,

and then deposits what looks like the flash
of a signet ring into the water –
his hollow beer-can lands without a splash.

I don't look up, rather I watch the shoal
jolt with that vibration, and jump like nerves
startling their own reflections back to real.

Surfers

Couched in a recess from the wind I've seen
ravens fly back and forth to this cliff-ledge,
and watched the sea returning, and its sheen

turn bluebottle-blue flecked with indigo,
as though ink dropped into an abalone
accounted for that darkening. The flow

is rapid, and surf blazes across flats
burnished a hard gold by the wind, ribbed sand
planed level as a sheet of glass. In hats

and beach shorts, the surfing crowd congregate
beneath the sea wall, and out of the wind,
absorb the sun's fierce energies, the slate-

like textures of their bodies oiled to bare
both sea and sun. Up here I watch those birds
drop down through a blue crystal of sea air

and comb beached drifts of wrack dried by the heat
to fossil strands where flies fester. Each wave
asserts a resonance – a drumming beat

communicated to the group who tan,
awaiting a heavier lift of surf
to call them to their boards. I watch a man

squat down, his pulse picking up the rhythm
of each new smoking wall of surf that gains
momentum, shot through with light by the sun

to subside with a mulling poker's hiss.
He's like a sentry in his black peaked cap,
maintaining vigil, and at his raised fist

the word is out, and down the beach they race –
these tiny figures running with their boards
into the wind and the blue rim of space.

Visiting Hours

I try to reach you who reverse in years
to a child lost inside a labyrinth,
and it seems you're my son now, not father,
and it is I who must answer questions
by a frightened bedside, and allay fears
that root in you, and by circumvention
of facts, pretend that it's an interval

of rest you're here for, not a terminal
illness; and that this bed, this window pane
dustily framing the roofs of London
is the last corner that you'll come to know
on earth; the ward for four, circumspect walls
of white, the soundless television screen
that's on all day, and the routinal pills

that deaden your cancer's anabasis,
steroids to reduce brain inflammation.
Fifty-eight years without a day's illness,
and now your helplessness is of a child's
fumbling for speech, for a balance that's gone,
and leaves you without co-ordination,
seeking sleep, like a diver gone on down

to find an exit that was always there,
but never used. Each day you go deeper
in that exploration, while we in air
can only call you from a great distance,
and meet you when you surface. Who's farther
from whom? I only know you need me here,
as once you comforted me in nightmare.

You hold my hand as though I were a spool
playing you out lifeline with each visit,
hoping that thread's unbreakable. Your pull
is vibrant at all hours, and the welts cut
each time you awake to panic or fear,
and I can sense your knowledge that you are
a hooked salmon who can't jump from the pool.

The prospect narrows. Standing in the sun,
I see my own death frozen in a beam,
as it will isolate me years later,
and I without offspring. You are my son
in these last weeks. A huge jet lifts over
the city; then the ward reverts to calm.
I too fear the end of visiting hours.

Housman in Old Age

The water's cold not tepid: an austere
face inquisitively feels the razor's
smooth passage induce no sudden bristle
or discomfort. (Once your criterion
for the awesome chill
attendant on a poem's inception.)
A long dormancy's blunted your response,
and if the razor slips, it's clumsiness,
not the sudden impulse of a lyric.
You've mellowed to a specious scholasticism,
and a bachelor's eccentric Cambridge walks.
Such is the age of one who wrote of youth.
The wasted years bay you like a gaunt wolf.

Rifts

in memory of Eugenio Montale

The ivy leaf's a diamond-lit frog's back
after the sudden impingement of rain,
and drops ricochet from the waxing black

of the sloe-berry, and the queen of hearts
is multiplied on each fallen pear leaf.
If a bird drops down it's quick to depart,

its eye flashing faster than a raindrop,
and coloured with the premonitory South.
The woodlouse locks fast in the log's slow rot.

Alive, you followed rifts, a kingfisher's
brilliant flare igniting the slow pool,
then imperceptibly lost in azure,

or the smoke spiral of a ship's funnel
hanging in a slow S while mist dispersed
to a rainbow. On cobbled flats runnels

tingled with light – each sea-pool a mirror
pointing you to the still more vibrant stars,
and sitting late the porcupine's tremor

was the first hint of storm, as a fish net
lifted by the gust concurred with lightning.
All life's the startled bolt of a mullet

disturbed by a shadow and gone so quick
we think it forever in migration.
You watched for breaks and knew the erratic

wavering of the sea-bound butterfly
touched on the very pulse of light, and drew
from its frenetic course a harmony

all light-borne creatures have. Word after word
catches fire in your work as mist singes,
and through its red hoop darts the migrant bird.

Summer

after Eugenio Montale

The kestrel's filtered shadow leaves no trace
on dry bushes, but tricks a darkened cross
on the heath's green awakening with spring.
The earth reflects the blue mirror of space.

Now that the year returns, perhaps you too
Arethusa show in the twisted gleam
of a trout shouldering upstream,
dear child whom death plucked from your fragile web.

Things catch light in a blaze. A shoulderblade
burns like a nugget exposed to the sun;
the cabbage butterfly flickers, a thread
suspends the spider over boiling surf –

and something imperceptible quivers,
and won't pass through the needle's eye, but burns . . .

Too many lives are needed to make one.

New Stanzas

after Eugenio Montale

Decisively you extinguish the last
red tobacco shreds in the crystal dish –
an heirloom left over from your rich past,
much as the retinue of your chessboard,
ivory knights and bishops will outlast
the sinuous smoke spirals you dispel
ceilingwards, a mist that obscures the hoard
of knuckled gold that burns on your fingers.

The heaven-sent messenger who disclosed
ethereal cities of the rainbow
to you in reverie has disappeared.
Your eyes snap back from that unseen window
to agitations of smoke, and a pack
of troubled thoughts bred by the underworld
clouds the features of each heraldic face.
You wear fear like a mule a heavy pack.

Watching you thus, I doubt whether you know
what game is played beneath you on the square.
Chain-smoking, you set up a beacon's glow
against the marauding black wolf of death.
Your vigil shows this, and it's in your stare,
a lightning awareness of other fires
staked out around you in the pit below.
You sniff their embers and await the flare.

The Eel

after Eugenio Montale

The eel, that cold-water siren
migrating from the Baltic
to our warm Mediterranean,
is streamlined to resist the flood
in foment, and keeps low, its quick
malleable pokerhead, snaking
from hairline to hairline crevice,
working upstream, so sinuous
it might pass through a wedding ring,
at last reaches the coppered light
filtering through green chestnut trees
and lies there, fired to a tabby
cat's orange markings in water
slowed from rivulets that streak across
the Apennines to the Romagna;
and contorted to a whiplash
catches fire like a pitch-arrow
in the arid craters left by
drought where mosquitoes simmer,
suddenly adopts the storm glow
of a spark that points to how
embers quicken in their extinction
round the stump of a dead tree-bole,
and how the brief, iridescent
blazing of its tornado flash,
is twin to the one between your eyes,
mad sister finding like a moth
ecstasy in the flame's surprise.

Amen

after Georg Trakl

These might be Dürer's hands clasped tight in prayer,
consigned to yellow in an old mirror,
the way sweat cools upon dying fingers
before they freeze. Whoever left these here
was icelocked by the blue of opium,
and left his ghost to brood like Azrael
at twilight over the autumn garden.

Persephone

The blue iris streaked with its pheasant's gold –
a sunspot foxing its deep-violet blue,
was what her eye alighted on, the cold
still snowing goose pimples upon her flesh
where she'd bathed in the stream's issue,
a goblet-shaped pool hidden by dwarf pines,
where the crested hoopoe perched on a spine
of rock and sang, and the kingfisher's flash

was like a turquoise shooting-star. Her hands
and feet propelled her with a swimming bird's
motion in water, she who'd had to stand
for hours in front of a mirror to learn
she was of earth, and overheard
the stream's insidious concourse, its bright
current would weave her veins into clear light,
or leave her an illusory heron

composed of water-spray upon a stone.
She'd left her friends paddling, and crossed a glade,
preferring to seek flowers, and hear the drone
of bees alighting on white narcissi;
and didn't see that sudden shade
darken the earth, as though the sun blacked out,
to be answered by an underground shout.
Its echo thunderclapped in the blue sky.

Before her stretched a plain, and asphodels
and the mauve crocus were a coloured rain
entrancing her to stoop, and white umbels
of hemlock caught the breeze. It seemed a jar
had been fitted over the plain,

for not a bird called, and she stood frozen
above the earth in a windless vacuum,
then fear was blinding her with a red star –

as a hairline zigzagged to a fissure
beneath her feet; his grasp was like a thorn
that went on growing to a tree, and where
she placed her hands blood ran, and tiny beads
speckled the iris, and the corn
shoots thrusting sunwards. Her head was a cup,
a rapid poured into, breaking it up,
and when the pain subsided, then her need

to know its source was quickened, and she fell
plummeting into a pitch-black spiral,
flight after flight through a vertical well,
his glowering eyes above her, and his knees
pressing her rump into a ball
that twisted in its drop, and when she woke,
her hair was singeing, and she clawed through smoke
to where a dog howled beneath cypress trees,

and found him staring into a mirror
in which nothing showed but a cobalt star
which changed into a man in a tether
hanging upside down. She was turning numb
and felt the pain cool in the scar
he'd opened in her; air shot through her veins,
and she was kiting up above a plain
where men cast crow's shadows, her mouth locked dumb

and leathery before he held the red
fruit of the pomegranate to her lips,
and watched her bite it until her mouth bled,
that sharp sacrament promising rebirth

as a blue shadow of the pit,
but already she knew she would reclaim
her heritage of light, and in spring rain
finger the green shoot thrusting from the earth.

Elegiacs

I

A bay so iridescently becalmed
one could have used it as a mirror to
paint a self-portrait. Mullet in haikus
lipped frond: their browsing chimed like bone china
on the water's ultramarine surface.

II

August: we came here the month of gorse fires,
outsiders bronzing naked in the coves,
the sand ribbed like a fishbone. The others
kept to the near shore, burnt bark-brown in oil.
Everything touched crackled with a red flare.

III

Hazed over, mist was the first touch of chill
in a sea garden plumed with pampas grass.
We huddled. The quincunx of a rock pool

29

was what I thought of, its bright mosaic
an ordered sequence winter tides would cull.

IV

So soon estranged. We stood above the bay,
and watched a flight of martins dip the cape,
and bend into their migrational pull.
We left: two in flight, anxious to escape,
our separation ringing like goats' bells.

Death Bed

after Po Chü-i

My bed is placed by an unpainted screen,
and sunlight filters through a blue curtain.
Those rapid voices are my grandchildren
inflectionlessly reading me a book,
while I pencil amendments to poems
sent me by friends. Drug-money, and a cook
to heat me wine are my small requisites.
I'll die facing South and facing the light.

To Him Away

Today, our son, my Lord, was much estranged,
   being most lately come
from Gheel, where certain wandering madmen
impressed his youth with black omens,
   so that he walks with tonsured head,
or broods distractedly for hours
   upon the progress of the sun.
I fear he is no longer ours

in sense, and pleasure's to him alien.
   He keeps himself above
a young man's passion to despoil or love,
and is a hawk become a dove.
   I fear the promised union
with Sherbourne's fairest is amiss,
   and increase of estate removes
itself. My Lord, I do distress

you, that I know, you being at the wars,
   and rain making a churn
of every country road. Doubtless we turn
to grief most when there's no return
   by messenger or brumous prayer
I despatch in our cold chapel,
   asking of Christ to move our son
into the light, who strangely fell

into this restless torpor. James, my Lord,
   came speaking with half your
tongue, and half his, as becomes a brother,
and thought to let blood would confer
   upon his nephew quietude.

The need is pressing, for he speaks –
   and this alone gives him pleasure –
of making gold in a retreat,

as lately certain charlatans perform.
   I ask you to renege
all lands promised to him when come of age,
rather, I risk, my Lord, your rage,
   by writing I forbid. Your scorn
at first must not cloud your reason.
   Think, landless, nothing would assuage
your broken pride before the Queen.

The evening bell, and I must late give seal
   to this troublesome news.
I beg you ponder how your son eschews
all reason, before you review
   with what physic we may expel
the mad forebodings of his brain.
   My Lord, as we, pray for our souls.
I send you good tidings: your Jane.

An Age Bereft

for Philip Smith

They won't recall our panache, our finesse,
we're outsiders in an age without Proust,
James or Cocteau to notate how style is
a something-not-pronounced, minutiae
of speech, the angle of a handkerchief,
a buttonhole or orchid in a vase,
a mauve ink inscription on a flyleaf;
but more a sensitivity which holds
each mind invulnerable in its privacy,
unencroached on in areas which flinch
a lifetime with the fear of exposure.

                              Rilke, a rose
pressed inside a green vellum book evoked
centuries committed to a girl's diary
by her writing posthumously at a yellow
lacquer desk over which a bee wavered.
A lifetime lived extracting essence like that bee
from moments of evanescent selectivity

is what we look for, the few who remain
divided by a spiderweb from threat
of extinction, recall an autumn night
on an unclouded lawn reading poems,
each knowing it could never be the same
surprised by a red adventitious moon.

Barn at a Tilt

A blue arrow of sky chases across
the brushpoint pebbling of uniform grey;
wet blackberries wear diamond pins of light,
and sparkle like the jet bead of the bay

on which a dinghy cuts a white spadehead
of foam. You've parked your car beside a barn
in which a poet summers with swallows.
A robin taps out a code of alarm

on the tabby markings of a snailshell,
and the rising moon's a sanded mirror
already frosting with its flatfish spots.
We walk towards the headland and defer

speech for reciprocal intimations
of a valediction tightening like wire
around the sinews of a rabbit's paw.
On the heathland someone has lit a fire,

and its subtleties recall gradations
of years cast like pebbles into a well,
so clear that I can see and count them all.
They fidget with the tremor of a bell

the surf rocks. Space becomes our only goal,
walking as though the air was a springboard
projected from the cliff. A bat dipped by,
noiselessly voicing its hunger abroad –

and still without speech we came to the edge,
startled by the blustering of someone,

white-shirted, tieless, the out of season
poet storming his thatched barn at a run.

Sea-room

1 Mazarine, and at dusk the holly-blue
of that frail butterfly pinned on a light
of dusted persimmon became our view
at Rock Point, strangers who met in a crag,
fished by the dipping cormorant and shag,
both stripped to swim, treading water, upright
as glass-blue bottlenecks in that gully;
each stroke formed hemlock clusters on the sea.

2 Your ring, a scarab in mottled turquoise,
mirrored the sea, your matelot's striped vest
was scarlet and white, and gold sparks of gorse
were saffron scallops caught inside your shoes.
We sat, tented in towels, scoured by the blue,
both solitary, two blown leaves at rest
beneath this cliff, where the gannet's poker-
dive resurfaced with a mackerel's quicksilver.

3 A room in which two leather jackets hung
upon a nail; a frugal whitewashed shack
above the breakers, where a bell-buoy swung
with the tide's rhythm. A cindering heat
had us dare surfaces with blackened feet,
running down to the shallows, where a slack

tide's enervating kitten-ball of sleep
fluffed up a white swell on the coal-blue deeps.

4 Two strangers, fuelled by a wasp's energy
to sip at every pollen cup, we grew
delirious at small things, while the sea
clouded from manganese-blue to peach-grey,
and small fishing boats piloted the bay.
At night on the jetty the lobster's blue
claws were tied, spidercrabs, shankers, their slow
grind in a sack was a commando's crawl.

5 This flux and ebb, a sea-change like our moods,
mercurial, and drawing back from trust,
distempered, like a spider left to brood
outside its web, for fear it shatter it.
At low tide the rocks were a boiling pit
of water dragged out; flies brush-stroked the dust
that scalded on the cliff path. In terror
we waited for the moon's radiant mirror.

6 A night in which our shadows seemed to grow
too huge to control, and the ice-bright stars
so visible, it seemed a wind could blow
them to embers. Bacchic, crowned with ivy,
I thought I saw you by the wildrose sea,
blood streaming from your body's frosted scars,
and later found you fingering a stone,
its bird's-egg speckled clouding – a small moon.

7 They fly into the beam unwittingly,
nocturnal shearwaters the lighthouse man
throws back into the air for levity
so they regain their flight. We too struck blood
in a drunken rage, the tide at full flood,

your skin so leathered from its scorching tan,
I thought you, part man, and part amazon.
The dawn's first light was a pink carnation.

8 An empty nail; the seapinks in a jar
were all you left, their crowns studded by dew,
and I returning found the door ajar,
the room so strangely light I knew you gone,
the window catching crimson with the dawn
then mauvely erupting to cornflower-blue.
I sat and counted the seapinks, and heard
my blood beat with the outcry of a bird.

Lumber Room

The dark inside smelt of convolvulus
gone musty after rain, and a pappus

of dust thistled each cobweb's tarnished watch-
interior. Light let in by the latch

was a diamond ray tapped out to a code –
a migraine to the spider's eyes to goad

it out of its lilliputian parasol.
Inside, I listened to the martial roll

of small disturbances, and a soot-fall
of air moved with me. It was ritual

this going back upon a scent to find
a burial enacted in the mind –

a child standing before a cracked mirror,
its irezumi mask of bright colours

a solitary Noh drama, while the rain
was a horse's tail swishing flies, a stain

that mouldered in the rafters. Turpentine,
old jaundiced books, tied up trunks, and a wine-

bottle with stalactites of wax were my
discoveries, familiar genies

for a child's magic, listening to his thoughts
name symbols for their colours, while the knot

of the bunched spider stirred like breaking ice
inside the thumb-screw pincers of a vice.

Two

They turn their backs to me; the father's eyes
are crushed blue ice in glass marbles; he flies

his son's kite with one eye into the wind
and one restraining the child who scuffs sand

in a tantrum. Something is very wrong,
the child is disproportionately strong,

his shaved head, concave nose, and dribbling mouth
suggest a mongol. Panting in the drought

of August's sun-kiln, his orange lolly
planted in sand is like a melting tree

that he's abandoned. Crows keep flying back
and forth across the beach, spading at wrack

for what the sea has jettisoned. I watch
the ritual of these two; the shaky match

scratched with one hand the father clumsily
keeps trying to light while observing the sky

with a strained concentration. The child grins
as though his mouth was open on a pin,

his spittle congealing to stalactites;
and now the kite is gusting and its flight

attracts attention. He runs after it,
pursued by a mongrel who jumps to grip

his wrist, and keeps on pulling till it bites.
The father sits back; his cheroot's alight.

Dead Hand

His dead hand catches, while the right secures
clothes randomly discarded on a bed,
garments he's seen worn once or twice before,
but kept in store, that velvet suit and red

silk shirt, the water reflections of ties
contrasting lapislazuli with grey
shot silk – vestiges of a taste that lacked
courage to wear them, now exposed today

on counterpane and floor, a mosaic
to be boxed up and sent to charity
bazaars. His right hand's an inert puppet
that needs constant attention as though he

composed all movement to accommodate
its handicap, nursing it to repose
on safe surfaces. Cautiously he swabs
a thin red line issuing from his nose,

and addresses the empty room, while cold
sunlight whitens the pane, and forms a star
diffusing itself in oblique sunbeams.
He thinks, how in seconds he's come so far

towards the edge of being, that he knows
all time encapsulated in one stare,
and composed of his loss. His dead hand drags,
as on one knee he faces the harsh glare

of sunlight, and tucked beneath his good arm
a bourbon bottle's cradled. Down below,

41

the reverberation of stalled traffic
makes him conscious of the open window,

he slumps by, quickened by the frosted air,
and looks across at a removal van,
and concentrates on its blanketed wares,
his dead hand gummed to an open paint can.

A Location

It seemed part of an aerial photograph,
hatched in with blue and red tessellations,
and somewhere central, a black reservoir,
or place it the other way round, the hole
is in the sky, but not facing the earth,
and those hatchings are perhaps jet vapour
building in space a defence location

or fuelling-rig. Both are conjectural,
and Dwight, who flew a private monoplane,
surveyed the coast around, marshland and shore,
but found nothing improbable, no bore-
hole, nor Ministry of Defence sky-well –
aircraft had been known to clean disappear
before our eyes, then years later return,

pilotless, nosing down upon the dunes,
their body metal eroded by rust,
but of that time-fissure, we had no clue,
and thought of it as extra-sensory,
some pick up on the pilot's brain rhythm,
wrenching the aircraft up, but how it flew
was the enigma, for all lives were lost,

and no astrophysicist determined
correlatives between our coast and sky-
ceiling. Each day we'd hear Dwight's plane survey
our coastal purlieus, and patrol the bay,
looking for something we had come to dread
as right beneath our feet, but to our eyes,
invisible. We'd used telepathy

as a means to communicate secrets,
for centuries, and sometimes the flashback,
or failed intersection, would in seconds
so alter a man in body and mind,
we didn't know him, and this constant threat
was always with us, and in the beyond,
that so preoccupied us with its black-

holes, and temporal traps. We tried again
to find an ordnance survey that might show
parallels with the photograph we'd found
in a crashed aircraft; the panel surrounds
were still lit up, as though no lapse of time
had occurred, before its hitting the ground
without a pilot, and devoid of fuel.

And when Dwight disappeared that afternoon,
it came as no surprise, the midge-like drone
of his engine, suddenly extinguished
in the clear blue. We wished him quickly dead,
and knew we'd find the aircraft on a dune,
a week or month or year from now with red
and blue clouds round an upside-down black sun.

The Well

A concentrated bore-hole for the sky
this one has centuries of still brooding,

and a sharp kleptomaniacal eye
that tricks your features from you like a ring,

and reduces them to a cameo
a lilliputian shrinking. Afloat,

I'm poker-faced, and subject to the sky's
caprices, blurred like a face flaring up

behind a windshield in a blinding star
of sunlight. Peeka-boo Peeka-boo chimes

the head I am in its leaning over
inquisitively, and the rim is bean-

grey, chilled with perennial cold-storage,
no drought has ever consumed at its source.

If there's a bottom clouded with vintage
leaf-mould, mouthfuls of the wind's deposit,

its opacity would tarnish a rod,
but is otherwise settled in its bed.

I stay transfixed, the well's concavity
is textured like an unripe blackberry,

the walls tapering to an umbrella
that's rolled, and round it skirt drowsy horse-flies.

I rise, a man with distended knuckles
retrieving from ten feet a monocle.

The Chatter of Magpies

Querulous, hackingly raw; their chatter's
repetitious, ascending a scale
of rapid gutturals –
a football rattle devolving slowly
or a zinc bowl clattered by hail.

I listen at the wood's edge. Windy elms
lodge a voice gone with anglo-saxon-
heckling an old adage,
and now two gust up, dropping to hedges,
planing to stand tail-up on a stone,
or flick the liquid eye of a cow–bath,
nervous, as soon gone

to a footfall, one high to an oak–stub,
the other low down, luminous in the wind,
their incantation unriddling
the beetle's path, the snailshell's drum.

Conger

A conger's world is tubular, it means
seeing things thinly through a gun barrel
from the point of view of the bullet-head
that's primed to fire, the fist-sized, clam-tight jaws

more deadly in their lock than a bulldog's.
They'll shave a finger off with precision,
clean as a horse bite, or close round a hand
and leave it as taut gristle strung on bone.

The colour of beached wrack, or an old tom
that's greying, these inhabit wrecks, or lairs
from which their protruding head is streamlined
like a grounded jet's. Fastened to a spar

they'll fight on a short fuse, and savagely
bite free of suction pads working to grip
the powerful torsion of the body's girth.
In biting, their mouth opens from a slit

to an alsatian's wide full-toothed gullet.
Conger stay low, anchored to the sea-bed,
solitary killers holed up in their dens,
they mostly go unchallenged, like this head

which would swallow a sewer-rat or cat
washed out to sea; engorge it, and lie low
until nightfall, and then seek out new prey,
killing with a psychopath's will to slow

the moment to all time. Dragged to the air,
a conger barks, and if not killed outright

will live a day, and still retaliate.
This black boothead dazzled by a boat-light,

come loose of the hook, might jump at a throat,
and drag a man down, who stands shrinking back,
petrified at this one to one combat;
a jerky lighthouse twitching through the black.

Dogfish

A sensibility of teeth; down there,
plumb-bottom, where the light is diffused smoke,
and what moves dares that green opacity,
is where one finds you, your round toe-capped snout

raised at the height of a rat-trap from sand
shelving to stone where the conger's snake-head
stokes in its rock lair, and decapitates
an unsuspecting wrasse. What are the dead

to the sea's predators – the millions
of carrion subsumed daily, eaten
before they're dead, or falling to the depths,
scavenged? Nothing has time to go rotten

or stiffen out. The sea would eat the sea
if it had jaws, not the mere force of weight.
And this one, lacking a shark's toothed bonnet,
is still ferocious, and its gut a freight

of green crabs, wrasse, and the sand-stippled plaice.
Spotted, its desert-tank markings disguise
its basking, dredging the sea-floor at night
for flesh split open, fig-ripe, mauve. Its eyes

are set at a pig's angle to its snout,
a lesser shark, it is lobotomized
of the insatiable rip-cord to kill.
The one I hooked had never realized

that space is everywhere there isn't sea,
lashing out on the boat-boards, blinded by
a hurricane lamp, spotted like a log
coming to life, agonized with surprise

at a split-second world that's alien.
For man the reverse process would punch out
his oxygen, and cramped into the cold,
he too might cry, and pressure freeze his shout.

Mullet

A feather fall's a meteorite's crater
to these, so sensitive to sound, water

they pass through seems to chime; a leaf's tremor
will send them like a bird into cover

because a shadow's a predatory
antenna of the human eerily

preceding a foot's performing echo.
The light flares citron in the warm shallows

where mullet browse in a blue calm or bolt
out of the water – an exploding cork

exchanging elements in a rainbow
of vaporizing spray. Sometimes their slow

inquisitive brooding is like a cat's
translating everything to smell, their slate

bodies warily somnolent or gone
like shooting-stars should a shadow become

a superimposition on their sky –
a staining in of features that won't dye

the sunstruck surface of the world they seem
about to break through after lipping green

weed round a jetty or patting a bread-
crust clockwise round a circle. How they feed's

with the same delicacy as they play
with an angler's bait nosing it away

in pendulum fashion. A quicksilver
flash of a belly and the shoal shivers

like a glass breaking – and in bright splinters
converge as an arrowhead streaking where

the water's deeper, and with blunt lips scroll
the surface into liquid parasols.

Questionably

Questionably hexagonal, certainly mauve,
and not forgetting Officer, for courtesy,
is how I described the lenses and frames
of the getaway driver, how he'd left
                              rutted tyre-treads
in braking quickly, turning full-circle,
mounting the pavement for a hit and run.
It happened with that indivisible rift
between lift-off and the airstrip's contact,
                              you know that shift
that's not spatio-temporal, it's like
finding a mirror is not glass but sky
                              one's sucked into
and out of as phenomena that haunt.
We don't want metaphors but incident
came the reply, as I jacked a lighter
                              and remembered
one doesn't when talking direct to the police
interpolate speech with meditative
                              smoke. He did.
I would have enumerated but he
had lost the colour of his eyes, while two
green sequins sparkled on the black leather
                              of my passenger-
seat. I saw his mind figuring out how
to retrieve them without asking. Stretcher-
bearers hurried a red blanket over
                              the victim
and departed, and with them too, the crowd.
I knew a warrant to search my car would

be his logical tactic, but instead
                              he placed dark glasses
on, quavered, then shot himself through the head.
I had to resume interrogation.

John Clare's Journal

Conjunctivital, lame, his nose dripping,
I teach a poor boy and refuse his coin,
and would rather have him read Thomson's Spring
than pore over figures scrawled on a slate.
Outside it rains, and my chrysanthemums,
claret, canary-yellow, white, agate,
show double flowers; and it rains
over Helpstone, and mires the country lanes.

For months, uncommonly depressed, I've sat
and watched the seasons fail, and felt a dark
oppress me, and I've stared out like a rat
from a wood-pile, terrified when I die
my sins will twist like ivy round a bark,
and leave me a lost wraith. Sometimes I cry,
and fear my family's ruin.
Everywhere the red crackle of autumn

lights brief fires; crimson hip, haw, glossy sloe,
hawthorn, and plum-black bryony berry
are winter portents, and my asters glow
in their pied embers. The same pious books

arrive from Radstock, and Taylor defers
my proofs away in London town. A rook
fares better on sparse carrion,
than I the proceeds of my rusty pen.

And still they linger, Billing's late swallows
fan the burgundy air of October
and with their late departure, I'd follow
into the blue sky, and be free. My themes
are no more fashionable than Bloomfield's were,
and he too, starved. Twice I've risen from dreams,
imagining my children laid
out as corpses by a potato spade.

And now that seasonal star, the Michaelmas
daisy, shows in blue clusters, and yellow
ruffles of chestnut leaves stipple the grass.
The little harvestbell quakes in the wind,
ragwort and marjoram linger below
the hedgerows, and twist thin threads, like my mind,
that's racked and vague. Sometimes I see
my own double madly pursuing me,

and then I cower for days in a wood,
or take to the road with gypsies, broken,
and better drunk. A poet's understood
a century too late; men badger words
into affected grace, an unspoken
eloquence, with grammar a two-edged sword,
soon rusty, cast into a pool
where books are ballast for the ship of fools.

Twelve months to set a title page; small fame
for I who charm a lyric from the air,
and suffer quibbling editors who blame
me for my wrong spelling. In Lolham Lane

54

I found dwarf polopody, and read Blair,
and listened to the slow, fly-flashing rain
tinkle in the flood pits. Alone,
my mind becomes one with the grass and stone.

Better to be a botanist, and mark
each seasonal change, and what's peculiar
to one's native region. A huge crow carks
above me, and for three minutes I've timed
a snail's progress over a slender spar
of twig. Thirteen inches: a track aligned
without a shift to left or right:
such close-up conditions a poet's sight.

A coppled crowned crane shot at Billing's pond,
a gypsy wedding over at Milton,
or a rare white maidenhair fern or frond
distracts me from the melancholy hours
I sit and ponder over Chatterton,
or muse upon the coloured plates of flowers
in Maddox's Directory; –
the white peony and red anemone.

They say Byron uses a whip upon
whatever woman inspires him to verse,
and then hangs her up as a skeleton
for crows to peck. Humbled on a cart track,
my inspiration's more a wolf-eyed curse
that keeps me penniless, nosing the black
tunnels a mole snouts in my brain,
vacant for hours, and hatless in the rain.

I dreamt I died last night, or else I fled
into an unfamiliar country,
enclosure had parcelled off, and instead
of finding refuge, I was hunted out,

and forced to stare into a bear's red eyes
and dance with it on a rail-line. A shout
started me, and a bailiff's grip
on my shoulder, worked up and split my lip.

I sit, tussled as my limp hollyhocks,
and watch a beggar pass. Driven from farms,
men scavenge aimlessly; the gypsies knock
and fiddle me a tune. Today I fear
a black shape that has spindle legs and arms,
and grows to envelop the sodden shire.
I am a wart between its eyes,
and yet I blow a grassblade while I cry.

Rain

Suddenly I'm astigmatic,
the horizon's a fine paint brush,
each hair's width bristle multiplied
to a pinstripe commuter crush,

that slants diagonally as wind
shifts verticals to map hatchings,
then straightens back to curtain rods,
or needle lines in an etching:

we count each drop's munificence.
Rain multiplies like pennywort,
thumb-tacks of blood on a dry road
darkening to an oilskin, each rut's

an eye-bath for the sky to see
itself in a jigsaw pattern
all over a county, surprised
at angular-sharp reflections,

and how the earth's a mirror turned
over to expose a dull back,
unlike the sea reflecting each
nuance of the sky track.

And in its sound resembles sand
filtered into a human ear,
or torrentially voluble,
water slapping a dark pier;

each bead is like a pheasant's eye,
a rainbow skeined on a globule,
a moon-model to the quick ant.
The yellow pear beside the wall's

a lifeboat man lit up by spray.
The rain subsides; drip-drop drip-drop
a form of Chinese torture –
each flower's running on the spot.

Cliff Fires

By day the road's a sheet of hammered tin,
a quicksilver spine snaking into hills
above the cliff, and in the distance thin

curlicues of haze are chalk-dust powdered
on cerulean, and ignite at noon.
Crouched in the shade I'd watch nervous lizards

pulse in the heat, then bolt like forked lightning
into a maze of stones. Each tip of grass
crackled with current, and the kestrel's wing

cast a shadow so still it seemed composed
of the landscape, and not a fierce trip-wire
to bring that bird down vertically, its red

eyes bloody like sirloin. Always the reek
of char was imminent, a dusting blaze
that would cinder a heath, and then a week

later, strike with its circling fire elsewhere –
leaving as residue black rings of ash.
For hours I'd sit here squinting at the glare

as though I stared into a bright mirror
in which I didn't show. Sometimes a gull
would cry out in air that was a razor

polished to hairfine-blue. And when he came,
that strange boy on an afternoon when heat
made coals of pebbles, and the bee hung flame

on the gorse flower, I knew no surprise
at his arrival here, his shuffling gait,
dowsing the furze with petrol on the rise

above the bay, while overhead the sky
furnaced to white heat, and the kestrel dropped,
kicking up dust round the vole's tiny cry.

Stick by Stick

A stoked temper's a big cat in the blood,
and flickers of heat lightning tell me that
the imminence of your unleashed outrage
will suddenly strike like a ball a bat

sends crashing to the boundary. All day
the air's been touchy as a nettle patch,
and breathing in the sultry heat I smell
the crackle of a gorse fire a flipped match

sets blazing in crisp furze. If there's a leak
it taps like an oil drip on a wet road,
a blood-count spiralling to combustion,
so that the red fleck in your eyes explodes

to the wild bloodshot of an outpaced horse.
The room contracts, and its rice-paper walls
threaten to let the neighbours in; I hear
your fist beat a hornet's nest to a squall,

each irascible word, armed with a sting
that goes so deep, I come to doubt that we
are human in this combat, locking skulls,
squid-eyed, reduced to a monstrosity

we doubt as real, but think we act the parts
in a blood-letting; a wolf spider's itch
to entice the male to white sexual heat,
then pick its eyes out in a bone-dry ditch

before the rain storm floats both on the froth
of its torrential stream. We gag for air,

60

clumsy as seals, wading in divers' boots,
cumbersome, frazzled by the lightning's glare,

two wasps simmering over shattered jars
of jam, a broken chair, smashed tabletop,
licking our sores amongst that jellied flow,
too tired to go on, and too mad to stop.

Tulips

These have the reticence of pedigree
breeding, an overstrained, suave dignity

that keeps a poker-grip on things; a tight
refusal to open out to the light,

adamant, in their baronial excess
of colour, torch-bearers under duress

to hold their cool composure for three weeks
in strains of scarlet, mauve, crimson with streaks

of gold, flaming tangerine and dove-white.
Their haughtiness is nerves; each scion's fright

is premature collapse, the palsied shake
that starts a tulip's death; the centre breaks

to reveal a shell crater; each petal
resisting a quick coronary fall,

leaves six blackened candle-wicks as stamen –
a burnt out candelabra on a stem . . .

Tagged with insignias, Abbu Hassan,
Cape Cod, Dragon Light, they resist the rain,

immaculate, close-ranked, a furnace glare
of colour maintained with their special flare

to avoid thought of their future decline,
goblets revealing on both sides the wine

of their rich fermentation, while the bee's
their gold-striped headdress and emissary.

Snail

Is about strategical encampments;
    and is a cosmos to itself
with one inert survivor, not intent

on exploration, but lives snail-aeons
    in contraction, its antennae
closed down, its instinct to become a stone,

its tattersalled markings those of a grey
    tabby, and in its camouflage
inscrutable, is squat, sedentary,

odd like a parked invalid's bubble-car,
    and is laired up behind the dislodged
stone in a hole in the wall. Held askew

it's marzipan-green, or if picked hollow,
    the simple involution of
an ear's its likeness; grit rattles in there.

What are a snail's dimensions? The rotund
    completion of a smooth pebble,
all angularity erased: its mind

not even coming on in wet weather
      when its track is of white trefoil –
an oil freighter's slow passage of silver,

but antennae raised, a jelly-baby
      commando weighted down, but sure
of its passage, moving deliberately

to some inexplicable horizon,
      over a flatland bushed by moss;
its snipers taking refuge from the rain.

Air

Rain water brushed from a swift's pointed wings
on to an eyelash or a spider's web
is how I like to think of the exchange

of altitudes, a vibrant resonance
on this gusty day with birds ticking South
through a needle's eye, each propelled in trance

to dare luminous wind-shafts, and one feels
the elasticity of their wing-pull
in the air's simmer – the twitch of their pole

asserting gravity. The earth transfers
their arrowed passing as the aftermath
of hooves. I crouch down low and consider

the one vertical between me and space
that's flying westwards with the Atlantic,
and watch a singular whitewashed lighthouse

bulb on its rock. Out here the pulse of air
tingles with light hexagonals, I see
it transformed into design and colour

such as the intricacies a snowflake
contrives in fashioning its slow descent.
I sense those sharp intangible facets

pass through me, diamonding the light the way
hail flashes on a heated shovel's back,
or a cormorant's sheen glistens with spray

that smokes on its alighting. Sea and sky
in one illimitable rush of blue
open up light worlds, and the tern's shrill cry

untranslatable holds me static here,
given over to such fluidity
I am become a component of air.

Filming Couple

They've stayed on late; he writes, his guernsey sleeves
are holed; and in the land a shrew reddens
with the hawberries and galled alder leaves –

it might have been her car, back from filming,
she's conspicuous here with slashed dresses,
and careless of curtains when undressing

might be a cynosure for a voyeur
cat-flattened in bracken. One knows these things,
there's something wrong, the gin-empties are clear,

so too their emotions darkening like sloes
to distil an intemperate spirit.
She's made up for the Rose and Crown, and shows

a copiousness of flashy, fishnet leg,
but keeps a cool hauteur. He seldom calls.
He works at night or walks their collie dog

across the heath. They seem prepared to stay,
despite the summer's end, and back in town
their unanswered telephone's less each day

a hotline to openings, to filming news.
Here they're cut off, and if frustration grows
their rows are silent, or else kept so low

a window might vibrate without a voice.
Passing their garden I saw deaf-mute signs
become fingers leaving marks on a neck.

And then the grey one came, the director,
or so we learnt, and in pink cotton jeans
escorted her to the pub, his fingers

resting in conversation on her knee,
and unreservedly climbing higher,
and free of pocket bought generously

a last round of doubles for the locals.
Then she was gone; we glimpsed her last of leg
flash in her car, and watched the elm leaves fall

into its parking space. The men stayed on,
one writing filmscript, the other always
about to leave, but busy with a film.

The Person from Porlock

At first, there was no cause for suspicion,
the gentleman rooted in solitude,
had taken possession of a small farm,
and rarely showed. We'd seen him walk the lane,
encumbered by a trunk on arrival,
a scholar, so we heard, and indisposed,
given over to verse and reverie:
attentive about his despatch of mail,
perhaps distracted, but not sinister.

Then one night, woken by the discomfort
of a nagging tooth swabbed in laudanum,
I noticed that his light still burned; the shriek
of an owl scruffing a vole in the brake,
made me shiver at this man's blue candle
and protracted lucubrations. Women
on swearing fealty to the devil
had been turned into hares: confecting charms
was still a distillation of our parish

superstition. My wife wore a toadstone
to ward off ills that bedevil the noon,
and creep sinuously down the gnarled lane
in the shape of a black cat, or magpie.
I raked the whitened embers of the fire,
and huddled there, despite the summer air's
chartreuse and apple-green. A yellow moth
beat at the pane; and dawn was in the sky,
when she I'd left came down, and found me there;

but I disclosed nothing. Later that day,
I saw him scrutinizing the hedgerows,

where blue speedwell and the wild raspberry,
red dead–nettle, and the mauve dwarf–mallow
could be found by the contemplative eye.
His pallor scared me, and he seemed to look
backwards into his head, as though the sky
had made a compact circuit in his skull.
I hailed him, but he never once looked round,

only walked on in abstraction, and seemed
to utter words as an incantation,
and then retraced resolute steps back home,
and didn't show again that day. I sat
down on a stone and watched a goldfinch preen
the blazing pansy colours of its breast,
and found myself without the laudanum
to dull the viper in my tooth, so thought
to call upon that wayward, racked, person,

and ask the use of a strong anodyne.
I sat for hours in cold trepidation,
fearing to knock, and he, as though possessed,
scratched lines across a page, and when the pain
was greater than my own superstition,
I rapped loudly. He still appeared to dream,
and looked unseeingly right through my head,
as though the page was on the other side.
I said, there's something wrong, and grabbed his arm.

The Storm

A wasp's vibration in a gorse-flower,
that orange flame belling the wings' motion,
was how it seemed miles distant, the tremor

of a needlehead dropped from a great height
into the uncorked bottleneck we cooled
in a sea-pool. All afternoon the light

blazed iridescently ultramarine
on a sea surface fixed like an eye-glass
into the peacock of the horizon;

the hours afloat, and a torpid sea-bell,
leisurely tinkling; and you with a pen
and red ink, fashioned a memorial

to the dead seagull found upon the cliff
in our descent. A gruff buzz of black flies
sounded like a kitten's purr on the path

as they stippled that carrion. And down
below, the calm was eerie, and the lull
seemed like the sky and sea stood still, one calm

reflection, lacquered over with gold flecks
in lapis lazuli. We trod water,
or lay immobilely upon our backs

cushioned by the salt bay; and then it grew
this hairline of cobalt, to a fissure
of massing cloud, an ink-dot in the blue

expanding to a welled concentration
of angry mauves, and marbled quartz, and red,
and we could hear the thunder's vibration

stalk like a big cat growing voluble
behind the incandescence of its cage.
Then rain, each drop shiningly audible,

clopping into the sea, and shimmering
with a dragonfly's bright translucency,
each globule expanding to a white ring.

We took refuge before the downpour steamed
cleansingly through crevice and flaw, and smoked
skywards. You drew the lightning flares as red

unskewered spiral hairpins jumpingly
illuminating a cobalt skydrop,
while I saw the future, a butterfly

escaping its chrysalis, and on stone,
resting a while, before the longer flight,
sure like the migrant swallow of its home.

Giant Surf

for Michael Armstrong

We can't locate its place of origin,
this running wall, and its each successor
that breaks a mile out on a reef, then runs

at the gradient of a razor blade,
slightly atilt, and is the pilot wave
of that fomenting wreath of swell that's stayed

by opposition of a barrier,
and gaining momentum flicks the white crest
it inclines vertically, then waterfalls

into the wave's advance, and white water
boils dazzlingly at three times a man's height,
and expends itself in measured thunder

across the wide flat of Atlantic beach,
and in its outgoing rebuffs, but can't
impede, the next wave's towering overreach

that scuttles surfers, who in red and blue
attempt to choreographize each new
breaker's overhang, then fallen, review

the bay's slate-blue corrugations for that
one freak wave climbing to obliterate
the skyline, and on whose crest they'll lie flat,

pinpointing balance, vibrant in the light
of the spray's iridescence, until thrown,
they are towed forward, and surface to fight

the backlash that will wash them out to sea,
and winded, bask awhile in the shallows,
bodies aglow with that salt energy,

as though light formed a film on their torsos,
and left their flesh-tones a beaten silver.
They stand there, twenty of them, flecked with snow,

wading back into breakers, slipping free
into their element, while the sheer air
rings with each new wave's volubility.

Pendeen Watch

The kestrel's polestar in blue air
magnifies a pooled radius,
a death-trap lens to whatever
flickers across that treacherous
target-spot filtered to a ring
of blazing gold – the least quiver
brings that bird down upon a string.

On the horizon a white flaw
luminous as a mill–pond
reddens like a flame-tipped straw
the wind fans into embers round
a tanker's dead-squat biscuit tin,
and in that peacock's eye the squall
gravitates to a diamond pin.

And here where the Atlantic's bean-
green's turbulent with pitched groundswell,
I watch a rockpool's mallard sheen
cloud over like a darkened well
gulls drop into, and breakers grind
the cliff's underpinning, bracken
uncoils to goldleaf in the wind.

In a flash the bay's a mirror
reversed to show its blackened side,
blue mackerelings, and dulled silver
steam to a grey rain, and the tide's
mist with a voice. The foghorn wails
from the lighthouse, and a tanker
runs down the channel with the gale.

Around the coast from the Brisons
to Three Stone Oar, farm lights are on,
orange stars in granite hewn stone
eclipsed as the dead monotone
of the foghorn's cowsick bellow
goes out into the sky's frogskin . . .
Waves crash into the caves below.

And later the powerful white beam
of Pendeen Watch will nervously
punctuate the fog with sixteen
flashes a minute, eerily
shot through its quartz crystal prism
that revolves upon mercury.
The light transmits with a white hum.

I make my way back on a road
bubbling with rain, not a car-light
can wash through fog, squat as a toad,
in the warp of the Cornish night,
and shelter in a ruined barn,
as round the coast a flare explodes
and that red signal means alarm.

Outgoings

I

Immemorial the tern's cry
and the rain beading the haw
and the scarlet crab-apple,
eye-pupil bright crystals
on fuchsia, despoiled now
lilac and verbena, all
held in a globe of memory
poised to break like a rain star.

II

No finger-ring could hold
us, not sapphire or turquoise
on a thin band of gold
anchor the pulse. Rather
I'd be alone on jagged outcrop
facing the white Atlantic blaze
of surf hammered quicksilver,
askance like the petrel
daring the storm wave.

III

Sea-kale and sea-campion
their saline hardiness
sempiternally endure.
With us, a valediction
beneath a transient rainbow,

here today and gone
forever like swallows
unable to find a home.

Greek Colony

A sea the green of a butterfly's wing
idles to mid-ebb, and lazily oils
rather than runs. On dark reefs surrounding

the bay, men sunbathe in a mellow heat
that's gone by four o'clock in September.
Already small hotels are boarded up

preliminary to impending gales.
And if you don't come here, where do you go,
I hear the older say; they know the law

about establishing greek colonies,
and are more frightened how the winter long
they must live on the summer's memories.

Already they've thinned out like cormorants
when waters yield bad fishing. Some in twos
fidget, but aren't in pairs; the ugly can't.

I walk out, sanded by the season's dust,
and see the round blue metal beach-table
that crowned our rock, removed for fear of rust

erosion with the huge September tides.
Everything's disbanded or disbanding:
the season bodes departures, suicides.

Summer's like a roman candle, but brief;
the tan acquired, the grottoes sunbathed in
turn desultory like the red-edged leaf.

I watch a man dive off the furthest point,
and bask nakedly in the tepid calm:
the rock for warning's tipped with yellow paint.

And that reef's terminal. Beyond, current
insidiously joins the rip-tide's race,
and coastal beacons plangently descant.

We pour chilled wine into beakers and drink,
facing the horizon, the dunlins' shrill,
and beyond that, each his own personal brink

of fear and loneliness. Already waves
are heightening with the incoming tide,
and each still adamantly disbelieves

the end of summer, holds to the late sun,
like birds in migration, half turning back,
unsure it's not lonelier to go on.